Scholastic's

The Magic School Bus®

ON TV!

GETS PROGRAMMED
A Book About Computers

SCHOLASTIC INC.

New York   Toronto   London   Auckland   Sydney   Mexico City   New Delhi   Hong Kong

From an episode of the animated TV series
produced by Scholastic Productions, Inc.
Based on *The Magic School Bus* books
written by Joanna Cole and illustrated by Bruce Degen.

TV tie-in adaptation by Nancy White and illustrated by John Speirs.
TV script written by John May, Ronnie Krauss, George Arthur Bloom, and Jocelyn Stevenson.

ISBN 0-590-18731-7

12 11 10 9   1 2 3 4/0

Printed in the U.S.A.   24
First Scholastic printing, March 1999

You wouldn't believe the crazy things that happen in Ms. Frizzle's class! Like the day it was our class's turn to open the school. We came to school early and got our job list: ring the bell, unlock the doors, raise the flag, make up a greeting for the day, turn on the lawn sprinklers, set up the coffee machine in the teachers' room, prepare attendance sheets. . . . There was so much to do!

While we were wondering how we could do all those jobs, Mr. McLean came in with a humongous box. He told us that Mr. Ruhle, our principal, wanted us to set up what was inside — whatever it was.

You know how I said crazy things happen in Ms. Frizzle's class? Before we even opened the box, one of those things happened. Ms. Frizzle popped out!

Good morning, class!

Then she announced, "Mr. Ruhle's new super-duper computer has arrived!"

"A computer!" shouted Carlos. "That's it! We'll get the computer to do our jobs!"

Sometimes Carlos has good ideas, and this was definitely one of those times.

First we hooked up the screen (which, by the way, is called the *monitor*). Then we plugged the keyboard into the main part of the computer. We plugged in the mouse and the printer, too. Carlos turned on the computer. But it didn't do much of anything.

"Right now," explained Ms. Frizzle, "this computer is just an idle machine. It needs instructions to tell it what to do."

"But we don't know how to give it instructions," said Carlos. "What we need is a computer expert to help us!"

Boy, were we happy when the very person we needed wheeled into our classroom. It was Carlos's little brother, Mikey — the computer dude! Luckily for us, Mikey had come to school early to clean out his desk.

Mikey sure didn't waste any time. He started plugging cables into the computer. He told us to go out and plug the free ends of the cables into the bell, the doors, the flagpole, the loudspeaker, the sprinkler, and the coffee machine. When we came back into the classroom, Mikey told Carlos to record this morning's greeting. Here's what Carlos said into the tape recorder:

"Hi! How are you? Nice to see you! Thanks for coming to school, and enjoy your day!"

Then Mikey plugged the tape recorder into the computer, too.

OK, Mikey! Upload the workload!

Mikey started typing on the keyboard. We couldn't understand the signs on the screen, but he was telling the computer to do all our chores.

"Now I'll save what I typed," said Mikey.

Instructions written and stored!

On the screen, we could see a little picture of a school. There were also pictures that stood for each job we had to do. Ms. Frizzle told us that those little pictures are called *icons*. To choose a job for your computer to do, you just use the mouse to point to a certain icon. Then you click the mouse.

"Just click on the school icon and watch all your jobs get done," said Mikey.

We couldn't believe it, but everything started happening at once. We even heard Carlos greeting the school over the loudspeaker.

Ms. Frizzle was getting ready to send Mikey *inside the computer*! She put a set of earphones on his head.

"Now you can have your own guided tour," she promised. "And since the fastest way to get information into a computer is on a disk," she continued, "take a risk and make like a floppy disk!"

Mikey's chair started spinning around really fast. As it spun, it got flatter and flatter until Mikey turned into a disk! Then, like magic, the disk floated right into an opening in the computer.

We were still staring at the computer — with Mikey inside — when things got really weird. The school bell rang again. Carlos's greeting came over the loudspeaker again. From the window, we could see the flag coming down and going back up the flagpole, and the sprinkler went on right in Mr. McLean's face. The computer was doing all our jobs — all over again!

The next thing we knew, the computer [wa]s doing all our jobs *for the third time.* [In] fact, it was repeating our jobs *every* [min]ute! We were in big trouble now.

["]Let's go in there and get Mikey out [bef]ore Mr. Ruhle gets here," suggested [Ph]oebe.

["]Splendid idea, Phoebe," said the Friz, [get]ting that twinkle in her eye.

[Y]ou know our school bus is magic, but [did] I remember to mention that it comes [wh]en the Friz whistles? Well, it does.

We're going to be Frizzled!

We're going to be floppied!

I'm going to be sick!

We all climbed aboard the MSB — except for Arnold. He volunteered to stay behind in case Mr. Ruhle showed up early. When we all started to shrink, I began to think Arnold had a good idea!

So this is where the floppies go!

To the drive-in disk-o!

"A diskette, a daskette, the bus' turn into a floppy disk if we ask it!" sang Ms. Frizzle. I bet you can guess what happened ne

Inside the disk drive, a motor started spinning us around fast. Then something that looked like a long metal toothbrush began sliding along the disk.

"What's with the toothbrush thing?" Carlos asked.

"That's the read/write head. It's reading instructions and other information stored on the floppy disk," Ms. Frizzle explained.

"It will change the information on the disk into electrical signals and send it to the main part of the computer."

The read/write head was getting awfully close, when the Friz said, "OK, bus, do your stuff!" Just in time, the bus turned into a teeny blimp — with us in it! Now we had a really good view of the inside of the computer, but we couldn't see Mikey anywhere.

"Wait!" said Wanda. "Mikey was going to find out what happened to his instructions, right? And instructions are information, right? And the information is in those flashing signals, right? So if we follow the signals — we find Mikey!"

Would you believe that panels [i]n the ceiling of the bus opened, [a]nd skateboards came down for [al]l of us? If you've ever been in [M]s. Frizzle's class, you can [b]elieve anything!

Next thing we knew, we were [sk]ateboarding through the [in]side of the computer.

Time to skateboard to the motherboard!

"Wow! Where are we?" asked Wanda.

"You're skating on the cables that run from the disk drive to the motherboard. The motherboard is the heart of the computer!" shouted Ms. Frizzle from the blimp.

The motherboard was full of wires. And the wires were carrying electrical signals like the ones coming in from our floppy disk.

"This must be how information travels around the computer," said Ralphie.

Next the information led us to a big square thing in the middle of the motherboard. But still no Mikey.

"What's going on in there, anyway?" wondered Wanda. "It's all wires and lights."

Ms. Frizzle explained that the square thing was the part of the computer that's in charge of everything that happens inside.

"It handles every bit of information that comes in — *and* goes out," she said. "That's why it's called the central processing unit — or the CPU for short."

So Mikey must have come *into* the CPU . . .

. . . AND THEN GONE *OUT*!

Little did we know that Mikey was right nearby, listening to a guided tour through his earphones. Here's what it said:

"You have just entered the computer's random access memory — also known as RAM. A computer can't follow a list of instructions if it can't remember them. These RAM chips hold the instructions . . ."

Meanwhile, back at school, the computer was still doing our jobs over and over and over and over and . . . Well, let's put it this way: Arnold was not having a good day. Make that ditto for Mr. McLean.

But what could we do? We still couldn't find Mikey.

"Wait, wait, wait," said Wanda. "Mikey said he stored his instructions permanently, remember? So where does information get stored?"

"In the hard drive!" called Ms. Frizzle from the blimp. "It's over that-a-way!"

There he is!

It looks like he's going for a spin!

Mikey couldn't hear us because of his earphones, but we could hear what Mikey's tour guide was saying: "Welcome to the hard drive, where disks are hard instead of floppy. This is where information is stored so it can be used over and over again."

"We've got to get out of here!" yelled Wanda.

"No sweat!" said Mikey. "Computers send information out as well as bring it in. We'll just go out with the output."

"Look!" shouted Ms. Frizzle from the blimp. "There's some information on its way out to the printer now. Just go with the flow!"

Don't ask me how, but the whole blimp turned into a bunch of skateboards, and we followed the information to the printer. The Friz joined us and soon we were on our way out.

In my old school we printed, but we never *got* printed!

Boy, was Arnold ever happy to see us popping out of the printer!

Mikey went straight to the computer, while Ms. Frizzle explained to us that a computer isn't really smart. It's just a machine.

"A computer needs instructions it can understand to tell it what to do and how to do it," she said. "Those instructions are called a *program*."

"And if there's even one teeny-weeny mistake in the program," added Mikey, "everything goes kaflooey!"

And anyone can make a mistake — even Mikey.

I guess there's a first time for everything!

Mikey printed out his program so we could check it out.
"Let's see," he said. "Bell, doors, flag, greeting, sprinklers,
coffee, attendance sheets . . ."

It says "repeat every *minute*" instead of "every *day*"!

"No wonder everything is happening again and again," said Mikey. "The computer's doing just what I told it to do!"

"Which is all computers ever do," chimed in the Friz.

Mikey changed the word *minute* to *day*, stored the new and improved program in the hard drive, and we were up and running!

Just in time, too. Because Mr. Ruhle was on his way to our classroom!

"What's going on here?" he asked. "The school seems to be getting ready *by itself*!"

When we explained that the computer was doing our jobs for us, Mr. Ruhle looked mad. He said he had told us to set up the computer, not program it.

"Am I supposed to be pleased?" he asked.

Well, I'm not!

I'm thrilled!

I warned you about the crazy things that happen in Ms. Frizzle's class. Do you believe me now?

Letters to Mikey

(...ditor's note: They will help you tell what is real and what is make-believe in this story.)

Dear Mikey,
...y little sister's a computer ...niz, like you. She told me ...at you can't really see the ...ectronic signals in a ...mputer. I guess the ...ustrator made them ...sible just so we kids — ...d the kids in the ...ok — could follow them.

...s of Whiz

Dear Mikey,
We asked our teacher if you can really make a computer do your work for you, like you guys did. He said that since computers can turn switches on and off, anything that can be run by a motor can be run by a computer. Of course, the instructions have to be perfect — but you know that already, Mikey (ha-ha).

Smart E. Pants

Dear Mikey,
We once took apart a real computer in school, and the insides were much more complicated than the one you were in. The main parts were the same, though -- disk drive, motherboard, CPU, hard drive, and RAM. No blimp, no skateboards.

Noah Kidding

What's So Floppy About a Floppy Disk?
An Activity for Parents and Children

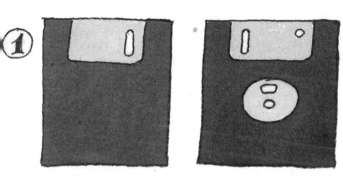

A 3.5" computer disk doesn't look or feel flop[py] at all. So why is it called a "floppy disk"? You can find the answer by "dissecting" a disk. (A[n] empty one!)

1. Look at your disk. What you see is really t[he] *housing*, or disk *case*. The disk itself is inside. The metal thing is the *shutter*. Slide the shutte[r] so you can see the disk underneath. The shutt[er] protects the disk when it's out of the compute[r.]

2. Use a butter knife to pry off the shutter. Then pry apart the two halves of the housing. (Don't worry if the housing breaks.)

3. There's the disk! It's the brown or black plastic circle with a metal center. Pick it up. See why it's called "floppy"? The metal center, or *hub*, keeps the disk in place while it spins.

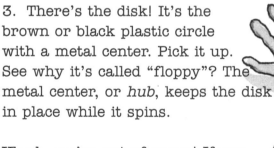

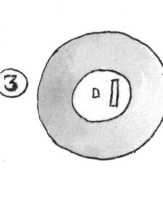

Uh-oh, we're out of space! If you want to know more about how a disk works, take Ms. Frizzle's advice. Make like a scientist and research! Look in a book about computers, or in an encyclopedia.

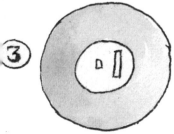